How to Keep What You Make

How to Keep What You Make

The Secrets of Money Management!

Robert H. Scott, Jr.

iUniverse, Inc.
New York Lincoln Shanghai

How to Keep What You Make
The Secrets of Money Management!

iUniverse books may be ordered through booksellers or by contacting:

iUniverse
2021 Pine Lake Road, Suite 100
Lincoln, NE 68512
www.iuniverse.com
1-800-Authors (1-800-288-4677)

ISBN-13: 978-0-595-39747-1 (pbk)
ISBN-13: 978-0-595-84154-7 (ebk)
ISBN-10: 0-595-39747-6 (pbk)
ISBN-10: 0-595-84154-6 (ebk)

Printed in the United States of America

Contents

Two Bonus Items Included!!

Bonus 1 describes the **Daily Workpad**, a technique which will help get your day's work done with less stress and added productivity.

Bonus 2 is **Santa's Secret**, a children's story about Christmas. Christmas is a one of the bigger budget busting times of the year. This story, and the way parents or grandparents can use it, will not only help keep Christmas in control but greatly increase enjoyment of the season. And it has a secret fun way for getting kids in bed happily and quickly on Christmas Eve!

Introduction

We all work hard to make our money. This book is designed to show you how to keep more of what you make. What's more…it will let you enjoy your money!

No more fear of whether you really can afford that new suit or new car or that cruise vacation. You will *know* what you can really afford! Maybe it is not a miracle but for many this system of money management comes close.

With the Money Management System you can manage your finances to meet your personal goals. All it takes is a little organization, incentive and time. The Money Management System provides you the organization. I hope it also will give you the incentive to take the time and make it work for you!

The author of this book has used the Money Management System successfully for many years and would not be without it. It made it possible for him to retire in his early forties. Twenty years ago, when his mother was widowed for the second time, the author set up a Money Management System for her. As a result she never had to return to work and for the last 30 years has stayed ahead of inflation. She swears by the system!

The author's son and daughter, one in a career in banking and the other a professor of economics, were the next in our family to use and benefit from the system. At first they were not exactly thrilled at the prospect! But, when they saw what it did for them…they *were* thrilled, believe me!

There is no magic in the Money Management System. Just plain common sense and a simple way to keep track of what you have and what it is doing for you. Follow the system and you will find you will be controlling your finances, not the other way around!

The Money Management System

What is Money Management?

Money management is the organization of your financial resources to meet your financial goals. Sounds technical? It really isn't! In simple terms, it means keeping track of what you have and controlling how you spend it or save it.

The Money Management System—MMS for short—is a simple record keeping system that keeps track of your spending and saving. At all times you will know *exactly* how much you or your family has to spend, and for what.

An Overview

To start, take a careful look at the Money Management System cards in the Appendix to this book. Look at the first card, "Illustration 1, Money Management Card" and keep it handy. These cards are the heart of the system. There are two cards. One is called the Money Management Card, the one you should be looking at now. This is the card you will use most; it will handle your day to day expenses. The other card, the Savings and Investment Card, is for your savings and investments. For now, just look at the Money Management Card.

As you work your way though the card, think of each expense category as an envelope. You _could_ cash your paycheck, divide it up and put the cash in different envelopes for different expenses—so much for car expense, so much for food and so on. The Money Management System works the same way, but instead of "envelopes" you will use expense categories.

Each week you will add money from your income to your expense category "envelope" and take money out of that "envelope" that you spend. Since you are using a paper record instead of an envelope during the week you will know at a glance at your Money Management Card just how much money is left in each of your expense "envelopes". Each "envelope" has a current balance. All the envelopes added together come to a total that is equal to your checking account balances and pocket cash.

Instead of a bunch of envelopes stuffed with cash, you have a simple one page Money Management Card with all your expense category balances in front of you. You will know what you can spend for what—without spending money you shouldn't. That is money management! **Before we start tailoring the system to your finances lets get started by first understanding how it works by looking at the system in detail.**

First, consider the headings:

<u>**Expense Category**</u>   <u>**Balance**</u>   <u>**Budget**</u>

Look at each of these headings. By the way, you will note that on the illustration there is listed **Current Balance, Subtract Expense, Add Budget and New Balance.** When we talk about "Balance" we are talking about Current Balance and "Budget" is the Add Budget category. Mentally for now just drop the "Current", ignore the Subtract Expense and drop the "Add" to Budget and ignore the New Balance. We will use all of these later but for now we want to focus just on Expense Categories, Balance and Budget.

Starting with the **Expense Category** heading. **Here you will find listed the categories of expense that fit your needs.** These should be detailed enough to permit you to see what you have to spend for each category of expense, but not so detailed to become burdensome. We are trying to make the job easier, not harder. The categories shown on the Money Management Card are only examples. Below, we will discuss how you select your own categories.

Balance—This column will show the total amount you currently have left to spend in each expense category. For example, if under "Food" you have $120.00 in the Balance column, then you have $120.00 to spend for food.

Budget—Here you will set out, by expense category, the amount you budget for each category of expense. If you have a regular paycheck this means the amount from each paycheck to last you until the next paycheck. At the start of a pay period you will add the "Budget" amount to the "Balance". The "Balance" column will then show what you had left after the last pay period plus this period's budget amount. Sound confusing? Don't give up! Once you get the hang of it, it will be easy! Just remember that riding a bicycle was hard at first but after once learning you no longer think about it and it is easy. Same with this system. Just stick with it!

Let's take an example that we will follow through this book that will help explain how the Money Management System works:

Al, an office worker, receives a weekly paycheck. His take home pay is $560 a week. He and his wife, **Betty**, have two children. **Chris** is age 4 and **Doris** is age 12. Betty has a part time job. She gets a monthly check that varies from $100 to $400 a month. They own their own home and have two cars.

Al and Betty have budgeted $120 a week for food expenses, which includes all food except Al's lunches and Doris's school lunch (these are covered by Al and Doris' personal accounts).

Last week Al and Betty's MMS Card showed the following for "Food" at the end of the week:

Expense Category	Balance	Budget
Food	-4.00	120.00

The minus sign means Al and Betty spent $4 more than their budget amount for last week.

They start the new week with $120.00 less $4.00 or $116.00 for food expense for last week. The card now shows:

Expense Category	Balance	Budget
Food	116.00	120.00

Al and Betty know they over spent last week and so have only $116.00 this week to spend for food.

Some Starting Ideas

Before you start making up your own Money Management Card, **here are a few ideas to make using the Money Management System easier for you.**

1. **Use lined notebook paper or accounting columnar paper** for your MMS Card to start. This way you can line up easily the expense category with the corresponding balance and budget. **We have included blank forms in the back of this manual that you can photocopy to use as your weekly form if you wish.** Any office supply store will have columnar paper (paper with columns for figures) and you will want five columns for figures.

2. **If you use a computer** and are comfortable with creating spreadsheets, this is a great way to create and keep your MMS Card. Even if you are a computer whiz you may still want to start with lined or columnar paper first and later put the system on your computer. And you will want to print out your worksheets to make it easy to update and to have handy to refer to them between updates.

3. **If you use paper, keep your card in pencil and use a Number 2 (soft lead) pencil.** Not only can you correct mistakes easily but you can keep using your card week after week without having to rewrite the entire card.

4. **Use an electronic calculator to do your math.** When I started using the system, calculators were few and far between. Now for a couple of bucks for a handheld calculator you can add and subtract easily. Better yet is a financial calculator which is just a little more expensive. Availability of calculators and computers makes the MMS really easy to use!

5. **Make changes on your card weekly,** no matter what your pay period. In between, keep a mental or a scratch pad record of expenses you incur. Once a week is a good time to update your system since more frequent changes are a bother and less frequent changes make it hard to keep control.

6. **Make changes on your MMS card at the same time that you do your other finances.** If you don't now have a fixed time each week to review and pay bills and update your checking account, pick a time to do these chores. Sunday evening is a good time for many people, others seem to like Thursday evening. The day isn't important. It is the setting of a regular weekly time to do this that <u>is</u> important.

Setting up your own MMS Card

Now you are ready to start. **The first thing to do in using the Money Management System is to set up your own MMS card.** As I suggested, use a lined piece of notebook paper or accounting columnar paper to start or probably easiest of all is the form we have included at the back of the manual for you to photocopy and use as your weekly form. A photocopier will let you enlarge the image to fill the page. If you use this form you may not have to set up your own expense categories or you may want to change ours to fit your situation. We have tried to think of usual categories but we know everyone is different. If you decide to develop your own MMS card then set up your headings as shown on the illustration card at the end of the book. **Be sure to include a space for the date you last updated your card.**

Expense Categories:

The next step is to select your categories of expense. There is no typical list of categories. Each person or family differs in their expenses. The illustration card is, however, an example that may help in selecting your categories. *Even if you are using the format we have provided in blank in the back of this manual we suggest you read this section since it explains the rationale behind setting up these categories and may give you an idea for changes you want to make to tailor the MMS Card to your personal situation.*

If you have a budget already this step may be easy for you—just use your present budget categories. If you don't have a budget, go back through your checking and other records for the last year and list your expenses, organizing them in logical categories. Again the illustration card may help. By using your actual expenses in the last year you will be developing a rough idea of the amount to budget by category. For now we are only concerned with picking out *categories of expense*; making up our expense "envelopes."

If you have access to Microsoft Money™ you will find they have a starting list of budget categories to create a budget on their system. The two systems compliment each other and you may find it helpful to use both. In particular, you may find their categories useful as you develop your own. For example, they break utilities down into various subcategories (e.g., cable, internet, phone, gas, electricity, water, trash) and include categories for things like day care which you may need. However, as good as Microsoft Money™ is, it unfortunately is a budget system that looks backward at your expenses and tallies them against your budget. What is different about the Money Management System is that you build up balances in your budget categories which act like mini savings accounts. So while most budgets,including Microsoft Money™, look backward you will find that with your Money Management System you are looking forward—with money already in place to pay budgeted expenses. This is a very different way of managing your money.

A look at the thinking behind the categories Al and Betty use, as shown in the illustration card, may be helpful to you in deciding on your categories. In setting up their MMS card Al and Betty first decided to bunch together shelter expenses, car expenses and other major categories, using specific items of expense under these major headings. Also, note that they listed expenses that are fixed and necessary ahead of other expenses that vary or are discretionary.

Let's look at some specifics on Al and Betty's MMS card. Al and Betty first listed their housing expenses. They own their home, so the first expense is for the **Mortgage Payment.** We put (rent) in parenthesis to show where those who rent would put that expense. Next, they listed **Utilities,** covering water, phone, electric and gas. The third category is **Repairs and Replacement,** covering such items as furnace repairs, roof repairs and the myriad of little repair expenses. If you rent you might not need this category or use it for building up to replace your TV, etc. Finally, they have a category for **Taxes and Insurance.** Al and Betty do not have to escrow these items so they set them up separately. These items may be included with your mortgage payment. If so, eliminate this category.

Under Car Expenses the first subcategory is Operating Expense. This covers both cars. It includes gas, oil, repairs, tires, and also Al's parking at his office. For a year, Al and Betty separated this account for each car. When they found it was just not worth the trouble they combined the accounts into one operating expense account. **Insurance** covers insurance on both cars. Finally, **Car Payment** covers the payment on Al's car. Betty's car is owned free and clear. They hope once Al's car is paid off to keep this expense category as a saving category for the next car. Eventually they hope they won't have to finance their car purchase.

The next several categories Al and Betty selected are self-explanatory so we'll move down the list to the category **Accounts Payable.** Here they list their charge accounts. As they charge items they deduct the amount of the charge from the appropriate expense category and add that amount here. When the bill is paid the payment amount is deducted from these accounts. This way they don't fool themselves in using their charges. This is an important discipline for anyone with charge accounts. The piper may be paid later, but it is accounted for now! **A good idea is to keep a separate columnar sheet just for credit card expenses with a cumulative total that you put in your accounts payable category.** This also makes a handy way to check your account when the bill comes. As the bills are paid subtract a payment on your credit card sheet, marking off the paid items and arriving at a new balance to put in your accounts payable category of expense. I suggest you use a columnar pad with 5 or more columns listing the date of expense, to whom and for what and having a separate column for each credit card you own with the last column for the cumulative total of all charges. Don't throw the old sheets away but file them with your credit card records, you may find this handy later if you need to check back on expense by date. If you spread payments out over time you will have to add interest as it is charged just as you would any other expense. **Your ultimate goal should be to pay off credit cards within the grace period and avoid interest charges. At current interest rates this is probably the best savings you can do. Most saving vehicles will not come near paying you the interest after taxes that you will get by not paying credit card interest.**

A tip for you in handling all those credit card and other receipts is to take a pad of legal sized paper and in the upper left write the year and a number for each sheet you use. You can then staple all those credit card, cash and other receipts along the edge of the sheet. Once the top is filled with receipts turn upside down and use the bottom. File these in a manila file folder. Then if you need to go back to find a receipt to return something, get warranty coverage or for any other purpose these are really handy. Once a year, around tax filing time is my time to do this, take all your sheets and along with your paystubs and checking records put these in a shoe box and file in bankers boxes for at least 6 years. I cannot tell you how many times having these receipts handy have made my life easier!

Returning to our expense categories an example may help you to see how these credit card categories are used. Last week Betty bought a new sweater for $50 from the Jones Department Store and charged it. When they updated their MMS card for the week Al and Betty subtracted $50 from Betty's clothing category balance and added $50 to the Other Account Payable category balance. The following week they paid the Jones bill for the month, which payment they subtracted from the Other Account Payable category balance.

The next category is **Savings.** Al and Betty keep $400 in **Emergency Savings** in their checking account at all times. They save $40 a week as **Other** savings.

This category on the MMS card "stores" the savings until transferred to Al and Betty's savings accounts. We will discuss in a moment how to fit your savings and investment accounts into the Money Management System.

The last category is Miscellaneous. Especially at first, this is an important part of the Money Management System. If you have accurately estimated your other categories this may turn out to be an extra savings account. If you run into some temporary, out of the ordinary expenses, this category will let you transfer funds from this category to the balance that is short.

Every budget needs flexibility. Most fail because they are too rigid. With the Money Management System you can make temporary transfers between categories without disrupting the budget. You can even have negative balances for a while in some categories—borrowing from other account balances that are positive. An example may help here too:

> Last week Al took his car in for repairs. What he got was a $200 bill for repairs he didn't expect. Al and Betty's car operating expense category only had an $160 balance. They needed that money for regular car expenses. Fortunately, Al and Betty had built up $200 in their miscellaneous balance. When they revised their MMS card for the week, Al and Betty looked at several ways they saw to cover the $200 expense—

> 1) They could take the full $200 from car operating expense, leaving a balance of -40.00. After adding the $30 budgeted for the week they would still be in the hole by $10.

> 2) They could take $200 from miscellaneous leaving the car account alone.

> 3) They could take from other positive balances to cover part or all of the expense.

> Al and Betty decided that since they expected to pay $40 for oil and lube on the car, the "extra" expense was only $160. Of this they felt they could

cover $40 more out of the car operating category. So, they decided to take $80 from car operating expense and the rest, $120, from miscellaneous. After adding the week's budget amount to each category, their car operating and miscellaneous accounts showed:

Expense Category	Balance	Budget
Car Operating Expense	110.00	30.00
Miscellaneous	120.00	40.00

As you can see, the Miscellaneous account smoothed out a potentially serious budget-busting problem.

Look now at the bottom portion of the MMS card. You will see on the illustration card the following:

Total	2,120.00	560.00
Less Al's Cash	50.00	
Less Betty's Cash	40.00	
Checking Account	2,030.00	

Looking from the bottom up in this example, Al and Betty's checking account balance ($2,030) plus pocket cash ($40 plus 50) equals the total balance of all the expense categories ($2,120). Al and Betty use only one checking account, a super now account that earns interest. With MMS they found they only needed one account. Had they kept two accounts the bottom of the MMS card might have looked like this:

Total	2,120.00	560.00
Less Al's Cash	50.00	
Less Betty's Cash	40.00	
Al's Checking Account	1,000.00	
Betty's Checking Account	1,030.00	

What about the pocket cash? An example will help to show how this works:
Last week Al had $50 left in his cash "account" on
the MMS card. During the week he cashed a $60 check
for pocket cash. At week's end he got ready to
revise the MMS card and Al checked his cash. He had
$40.23 left. Al ignored the 23 cents and assumed he
had $40 left. Adding the $60 check to last weeks'
balance of $50 Al had a total of $110. He subtracted
the cash on hand at the end of the week, $40, and Al
sees that he spent $50 in cash this week. Al kept a
rough note on his expenses on his calendar during the
week. He rounded these off to the nearest dollar and
he "guesstimated" his expenses in cash as follows:

Car Operating Expenses	20.00
Al's Personal Account	20.00
Recreation	10.00
Total	50.00

Keeping with this example we will also see how the "Checking Account" category is used. Also how the budget amounts are added to the various "balances."

After Al revised the cash portion of the MMS card, he
did the same for Betty's cash and then picked up their
checkbook. The following entries were shown:

Check Number	Balance Previous Week		$2,030.00
322	Food	110.00	1,920.00
323	Phone Company	50.50	1,869.50
324	Cash for Al	60.00	1,809.50
325	Cash for Betty	40.00	1,769.50
326	Master Card	150.32	1,619.18
	Paycheck	560.00	2,179.18
	BALANCE AT END OF WEEK		2,179.18

Al then started down the MMS card. He took the
balance for the prior week, subtracted the expense and
then added the budget amount. He penciled in the new

balance amount in the right hand column. When he is done for the week he will erase the expenses and will substitute the new balance for the current balance and will erase the right hand column. He will be left with his sheet now ready for the next week. At first this will seem awkward but bear with it and it will become easy.

For example, under Mortgage he added the budget amount of $50 to the old balance of $200 for a new balance of $250. Under Utilities he added the budget amount of $40 to the $150 balance and subtracted the $50.50 check (#323) to the phone company for a new balance of $139.50. After adding the budget amounts to the next several categories, Al came to Food. Here he added the $120 budget amount to the $120 balance and subtracted check #322, $110, for a new balance of $130.00. Al ignored the two checks for pocket cash since these were already taken into account. Al continued adding budget amounts to the categories until he reached the Master Card category. The balance here was $200.00 from which he subtracted check #326 for $150.32 for a balance of $49.68. Al ignored the paycheck deposit since that is included in the budget amounts he was adding to each category. Al continued through the rest of the categories. He then changed the Checking Account balance to read $2,179.18. The bottom of the MMS card now looked like this:

Total	$2,249.18
Less Al's Cash	40.00
Less Betty's Cash	30.00
Checking Account Balance	2,179.18

Now, before he checked the MMS card for accuracy, Al entered the date he updated the MMS card and put a check mark by each item in the checkbook that he

entered on the MMS card. This way, next week he will
know where he stopped the last time he updated
the card.

Al then added all of the category balances to confirm
his total. He came up with $2,249.30. He readded and
still came up with this amount. 12 cents off! Rather
than find his error, Al simply deducted 12 cents from
one of his expense balances and is now in balance. Had
the difference been significant, Al would have reviewed
his checking records and cash to see where he was off.
For less than $1 Al usually adjusts for these minor
errors.

Once Al was sure everything balanced he erased the
old current balance and the expense column and copied the
column headed new balance to the column headed current
balance. He now erased the right hand new balance column and
is left with a card with figures in current balance and budget. He is
done for the week.

You may be asking how you handle installment payments you may owe. An
example may help understand how to treat these items.

Al and Betty needed a new refrigerator recently. While
they usually don't buy on time, the store offered
favorable terms, so they bought it on a 12 month payment plan. On their MMS card Al and Betty set up a
separate expense category and budgeted the payment just
like any other expense.

Balances

We are ready for you to fill in the balance blanks on your own Money
Management Card. Now that you have established your own Expense
Categories you are ready to fill in the Balance column.

Start from the bottom up. Put your present checking balance on the last line.
Then see how much pocket cash you have and put that on the line for cash.

Now add checking and cash and put the total on the Total line. This is the amount you have to divide among your expense categories. *Before you make your allocation though, be sure to put the balances due on your charge accounts and credit cards in those the accounts payable expense categories.* Now you are ready to make your allocations. Once you have filled in all the category balances add all your balances and be sure they equal your "Total." Don't forget to mark your checkbook so you'll know where to start next week in bringing your MMS card up to date.

Budget Amounts

Once you have set up your expense categories and distributed your balances you are ready to allocate your budget amounts. The previous discussion should guide you in doing this. Be sure the budgeted amounts by category add up to your take home pay. Note on the Total line in the illustration card that the Budget amounts for all expense categories add up to Al's $560 weekly take home.

What to do when the budget changes?

What happens, for example, when Al and Betty's tax payment on the house goes up? They have to take from another account budget and add to taxes account budget.

What happens when Al gets a raise? They add the after tax take home increase to the categories they select and put the new total take home in the total line under "Budget".

What about Betty's second income? Al and Betty decided a long time ago they couldn't count on Betty's second income, first because it varies so widely and because Betty couldn't be sure that she would keep working. So, they have decided to save Betty's income for major purchases—new furniture, new car, college for the kids. As Betty's paycheck comes in they add her take home pay to the Other Savings category. When needed they transfer some of this to other categories that have gotten in trouble. They try not to do this though because they know it is a bad habit. After a couple of years with MMS they found they were making fewer and fewer transfers of these funds.

A Tip: If you find yourself continually "in the hole" on an account, one of three things is usually happening: 1) You have under budgeted for that category. 2) You are having unusually heavy expenses that will level out. 3) You are spending too much in that category. You have to see which it is.

If you are under budgeted, reallocate from a category that is continually flush, until you get in balance. If none are "flush", then you are probably spending too much overall. If answer 2) applies, transfer from a flush balance until the situation levels out or go into a deficit, making it up when the problem ends. If answer 3) applies you will either have to find added income or cut your expenses. **When you reach this point you are managing your money—that is what the Money Management System is all about! Whatever you do, don't give up! It will take a while to get the system in balance for you. Keep with it and you will be pleased with the results.**

We have assumed above that you have a regular paycheck coming in. If you have income that fluctuates (e.g., a retired person with dividend income, or an author with oddly spaced royalty income) you can still use MMS. I suggest in such a case that you open a savings account to which you deposit your income as it comes in. Then weekly, or monthly, withdraw an amount (as if it were a paycheck) from this savings account and deposit it in your checking account. Your budget amounts will then be based on the "paycheck" you have written to yourself. If you are a small business owner you are probably already taking a "draw" and that should be treated as if it were your paycheck. Of course you must figure out how much income you will have to spend each budget period (after allowing for taxes) and withdraw only that amount. You also will have to initially put enough in the savings account to allow you to level out your income. Think of your savings account as a reservoir that must always be kept at some minimal level, as cash flows in it is added to the reservoir and during the year the level of the reservoir goes up and down, but never below a minimum. Meanwhile each week or month (whichever you choose) you are taking a steady amount out of the reservoir for your "paycheck" to be added to your checking account.

Savings

Now that we have covered the everyday expenses what about long term savings and investment? The best way I have found to manage these is by a separate record I call the "Savings and Investment Card".

There is a sample card for Al and Betty at the back of this book. You will notice there are two sections to the card. **The first section shows what the funds are saved for and the second section shows where they are saved.**

Let's look down Al and Betty's Savings and Investment Card. The first item is **Permanent Savings.** This is Al and Betty's rainy day account. They are trying to save one year of Al's salary for a rainy day and are almost there.

Next is saving for a **car.** Al and Betty hope not to have to finance their next car and are coming along nicely here too.

College for the kids is still a way off, but not that far. So far they have only $4,000 in this account. With Doris only 6 years from college they know this must be added to over the next few years.

Miscellaneous savings they have allocated for next Christmas for a new bedroom suite they would like to have.

Since Al and Betty pay estimated taxes quarterly, the **Tax** account on their MMS card adds up. When it gets to $200 they write a check to their savings account, reduce the MMS card tax balance and add to the tax balance on the savings and investment card.

Finally, Al and Betty are saving for this year's vacation. They keep these savings earning higher interest in their money market savings account.

The Total comes to $32,400. Section II of the Savings and Investment Card shows that these moneys are kept in the credit union, U.S. Treasury notes and three money market savings accounts. The college account is in mutual funds that Al and Betty hope will increase in value when it is needed.

Of course, your Savings and Investment Card will vary greatly from Al and Betty's. This illustration should, however, let you set up your own Savings and Investment Card to coordinate your savings as well as your spending.

A Final Word

Make Money Management a family project. Let everyone see where the money goes and have a voice in where it should go. You will find that it is actually fun to watch accounts grow. You will stop worrying about running out of money at month's end after you have used MMS for a while. It may take some experimenting—and yes, some mistakes—to get yourself squared away and adjust your income and spending. **Above all, don't give up. Stick with it and you will master money management.**

With the Money Management System you are ready to take charge of your finances. You are ready to plan your expenses and have more fun out of the money you make!

Illustration 1

Monthly Management Card

Last Revision Date

Expense Category	Balance	Budget
Housing		
Mortgage (or Rent)	200.00	50.00
Utilities	150.00	40.00
Repairs/Replacements	50.00	12.00
Taxes & Insurance	50.00	12.00
Cars		
Operating Expense	160.00	30.00
Insurance	60.00	10.00
Car Payment	0.00	50.00
Food	120.00	120.00
Clothing		
Al	50.00	10.00
Betty	-50.00	10.00
Chris & Doris	100.00	20.00
Personal Accounts		
Al	20.00	20.00
Betty	20.00	20.00
Chris & Doris	10.00	10.00
Medical	20.00	10.00

<u>Recreation</u>

Vacation	30.00	10.00
Other	40.00	12.00

<u>Other</u>

Donations	10.00	10.00
Magazines	30.00	4.00
Life Insurance	80.00	10.00
Gifts	40.00	10.00

<u>Accounts Payable</u>

Master Card	200.00	--
Visa	50.00	--
Jones Department Store	40.00	--

<u>Savings</u>

Emergency	400.00	--
Other	40.00	40.00

<u>Miscellaneous</u>	200.00	40.00

<u>Total</u>	2,120.00	560.00
Less Al's Cash	50.00	
Less Betty's Cash	40.00	

<u>Checking Account</u>	2,030.00	

Illustration 2

Savings and Investment Card

Section 1—For What Are We Saving?

Permanent/Emergency	20,000.00
Car Savings	5,000.00
College Fund	4,000.00
Miscellaneous	2,000.00
Taxes	400.00
Vacation	<u>1,000.00</u>
	32,400.00

Section Two—Where Our Savings And Investments Are Kept

Credit Union	4,000.00
Treasury Notes	6,000.00
Money Market Savings—Al	10,000.00
Money Market Savings—Betty	5,000.00
Money Market Savings—Joint	3,400.00
Mutual Funds	<u>4,000.00</u>
	32,400.00

MONEY MANAGEMENT CARD				
LAST REVISED ON:_____				
EXPENSE CATEGORY	CURRENT BALANCE	SUBTRACT EXPENSES	ADD BUDGET	NEW BALANCE
HOUSING				
Mortgage/Rent				
Utilities				
Repairs/Replacement				
Taxes/Insurance				
CARS				
Operating Expense				
Insurance				
Car Payment				
FOOD				
CLOTHING				
Husband				
Wife				
Children				
PERSONAL ACCOUNT				
Husband				
Wife				
Children				
MEDICAL				
RECREATION				
Vacation				
Other				

OTHER				
Donations				
Magazines				
Life Insurance				
Gifts				
ACCOUNTS PAYABLE				
Master Card				
Visa				
Other				
SAVINGS				
Emergency				
Other				
MISCELLANEOUS				
TOTAL				
Less Husband Cash				
Less Wife Cash				
Less Other				
CHECKING ACCOUNT				
NOTES				

SAVINGS AND INVESTMENT CARD				
SECTION 1	FOR WHAT YOU ARE SAVING AND INVESTING			
	CURRENT BALANCE	ADD DEPOSITS	SUBTRACT WITHDRAWALS	NEW BALANCE
Permanent				
Car				
College				
Vacation				
Taxes				
Retirement				
Miscellaneous				
TOTAL				
SECTION 2	WHERE YOUR SAVINGS ARE KEPT			
SAVINGS ACCOUNTS				
Account 1				
Account 2				
OTHER ACCOUNTS				
Account 1				
Account 2				
MUTUAL FUNDS				
Account 1				
Account 2				
STOCKS & BONDS				
Account 1				
Account 2				
SAVINGS BONDS				
Account 1				
Account 2				

IRA ACCOUNTS				
Account 1				
Account 2				
401K ACCOUNTS				
Account 1				
Account 2				
TOTAL				

Bonus #1

The Daily Workpad

Introduction:

Now that you have learned to use the money management system to organize your financial life you may find another organizing system helpful. Properly used it will let you get more done and reduce your stress levels. Both good things!

I have used Daytimer^{tm} appointment calendar and similar products for many years. How someone lives without a calendar is beyond me. However, in addition to my appointment calendar I have found another unique product of use to supplement the calendar. I call this my Daily Workpad. Before discussing the Daily Workpad consider the following:

1. The Carnegie system is well known. Steel magnet Andrew Carnegie hired a consultant to help him organize and prioritize his life. The end result was a recommendation that he list 10 items for the day and put them in order of importance and then work down the list in order. Great idea but problem is that there are lots of little things that have to get done sometime but may never make it on the list, much less to the top of the list. Failing to do those little things (like laundry, groceries, paying bills) until they get to the top of the list is stressful.

2. The same problem exists with many other systems. They do not really help to guide you through a day or week ahead. The daily Workpad will do that for you.

What is the Workpad?

It is a spiral bound pad to organize your day, putting more important items on the left and less important items on the right. It has the date on top and various divisions on the page. The most important division is down the middle. Take a steno pad that has a line down the middle. You can use this as a work pad by putting the date on the top and drawing lines across the page at various intervals. For example, ¼ the page for morning, ¼ for afternoon and ¼ for evening. You can add lines for lunch and dinner if you want or just put these at end of morning and end of afternoon which is my preference. The remaining part of the pad can be used on the left for a "to do"(Carnegie style) list and the right for noting of expenses.

The line down the middle for the day divides very important (these go on left) from less important items (these go on the right). Perhaps an example will help. Let's say that on the way to work you need to drop off cleaning, pick up a birthday present and then have a meeting at 9 in the conference room. You also need to call and schedule your daughter for a dental appointment and order flowers for a friend in the hospital, and get gas. You need to draft a report that is due end of the week. You would begin on the right side by listing the cleaning and then the birthday present when you think you can do them. These could be done later in the day if need be and while not "super" important they need to be done. They usually do not make a traditional "to do" list. Then on the left side you note the 9 am meeting. Following that on the right you might list the two other items—dental appointment call and ordering flowers. These could slip to afternoon or next day so they go on the right side, not the left. Finally you would note the report on the left side with some time set aside for it.

For a long time I listed times on the left of the page but later found it was easier just to "spatially" organize these on the page.

When time permits I do the items on the right of the page. Often I move them up or down as time permits. If I get a few minutes I do them, if something interferes I move them down or to another day.

Having all items, important and less important, scheduled for the day helps immeasurably in relieving stress and getting more work done. By having days coming up on the pad as well I can schedule things in advance not only in the calendar but for the week coming up.

The key to the Workpad is having both very important and less important items divided by the middle line. Less important items (like anniversary or birthday presents) may not get you fired if you forget them but they have to be done. Even important items can be moved around.

Always use pencil to complete the Workpad . That way you can make changes easily. I line through the work done as completed. Gives you a spatial feeling of satisfaction to complete each item and check it off the pad. Life always throws us curves. The eraser on the pencil lets you easily correct and move items when unexpected things happen.

I know it sounds simple, but the daily Workpad is a real stress reliever and every bit as efficiency promoting a system as the Carnegie system. In fact the two, along with Daytimer^{tm} or similar appointment calendars work extremely well together.

Save your old pads and you will have a continuous reference back to things you did on particular days.

Monday July 1

9 Meeting in Conference Room	Set up dental appointment Call on birthday present Call for lunch reservations
Work on Report due Friday (2hr)	
Lunch at Trivoli with Pete and Samantha 12	Pick up birthday present
2 Interview new sales rep for Florida	Call Mary re dancing pick up Remind George about ball game at 7
Work on Report due Friday	
	Stop for gas before going home Pick up dinner on way home
6 Pick up from dancing class 7 Basketball game	
	If time: Laundry, bills due,
1. Meeting in Conference room 9 (1hr) 2. Report on Sales for June due Fri (2hr) 3. Interview new sales rep for Florida (2h) 4. Lunch on United Way for fall. 5. Dancing class pick up at 6 6. Basketball game at 7	1. Lunch $15 business ticket 2. Gas charged, $12.50 3. Birthday present, charged, $25

Bonus #2

Santa's Secret!

It is Christmas Eve—__the Santa alarm flashes__—Santa is near!

it is time for bed and quickly the children run happily to bed!

Enjoy Santa's Secret with your family this Christmas…
Santa's Secret is family fun for the whole season!

Bonus # 2 may seem at first glance an odd addition to a book about organizing your finances but Christmas is an expensive often budget busting and stressful time for many people. Especially for parents of young children. So anything that can help to reduce stress and increase enjoyment of the season can help your budget. Also, this little story and its uses with younger children will let you adapt the Christmas story to your personal values, no matter your religious convictions.

We hope that those of you with young children, friends with young children or with grandchildren will find this a fun way to enjoy the Christmas tradition

Parent's Guide to Santa's Secret

This guide will provide suggestions on the use of the Santa Alarm (to tell children that Santa is nearing their house on Christmas Eve) and on the use of Santa's Special Elves in your Christmas celebration. One of these Special Elves, Elf Earl, whose story is told in this book, has become a fixture in our Christmas tradition. We hope that the Special Elves will provide your family as much fun and enjoyment as we have experienced with our Elf Earl.

You can do as little or as much with the Special Elf as you wish. You can give the Special Elf assigned to your family your own "Elf" name and use your Special Elf to tailor the Santa experience to your own family values and traditions. The Special Elf lets you control the Santa experience, not the other way around.

You may only want to use the Santa Alarm (with or without Special Elf) on Christmas Eve as a way of getting children to bed. If so you will find it is a fun way to get the kids to bed, happily. If you have a fireplace and want to use the fire colors you will need to find a fireplace shop that sells fire color crystals. We suggest you experiment before Christmas Eve when the children are not present to be sure how much of the crystal to use. When you are ready for the children to be in bed send them to the kitchen for cookies and milk for Santa or on some other errand. Toss the crystals in the fire, then step back and watch their eyes light up when they return to find the fire ablaze in strange colors! They will be off to bed in a flash!

You can also use one of the light switches available at Christmas at most retailers. Used for indoor or outdoor lighting it has a small switch that can be pocketed and turned on remotely. Stanley makes one and retailers carry these regularly at Christmas. You can use it to control any item you wish to use as your "Alarm". When you are ready for the children to go to bed turn the switch on so the preselected "Alarm" turns on. You can use both the fireplace and the remote alarm, if you wish. Tell the children that there is a later alarm for the adults when they have to be in bed.

Be sure to have prepared the children for the experience in advance by reading the story and telling them what to expect in your home. Be sure to test the Alarm before Christmas Eve and you may want spare batteries on hand just in case. If you should have a problem, you can designate a special lamp in the room as your "signal." Unscrew the bulb in your signal lamp just enough to keep from lighting and let the children try to turn it on at the switch to see that it does not light from the switch. Then when they are out of the room you can tighten the bulb so it lights stepping away from it before they return. Needless to say, this back up is not as effective as a magical fire color or remote alarm that mysteriously turns on as a signal, but we have found children love the idea and are more than ready to "play" with the Special Elf story.

Before Christmas Eve you can use the Special Elf to have all kinds of fun with your children. Your family elf can receive Christmas lists, leave candy or small presents for the children before Christmas and otherwise interact with your children as you choose. We have even had friends who have had their teenage children, whose voices our children would not know, call as "Elf Earl". From what our friends tell us their older children had nearly as much fun with Elf Earl as our younger children. Use of the Special Elf is limited only by what you want to have the Elf do in your family. Whatever your religious or family values you can tailor the Special Elf experience to your family and its values, something you cannot do with the traditional Santa Claus legend. You control who and what your Special Elf is and does at Christmas time.

We hope that the Special Elf and Santa's Secret for Christmas Eve brings added joy and happiness to your Christmas celebration. We wish you and your family the most joyous of holiday seasons.

Chapter One—The North Pole

The North Pole never looked so good! Another Christmas was here! Elf Earl was tired. But he was happy too. He had just finished bringing toys to boys and girls on Christmas Eve.

What a good job he had! How proud he was to be Santa's very first Special Elf. Not many people knew of Elf Earl. At least not until recently. He always worked quietly, in the background. But now boys and girls around the world were starting to know about Elf Earl and all the other Special Elves too.

It all began a few years ago...

Chapter Two—Santa's Home And Workshop

It was a bitter cold night. Santa was quietly sitting before the fire. He was thinking.

Santa sighed and said, "How can I keep getting to all the children, Mrs. Claus!" Santa looked over at his wife. She was knitting in the chair beside him.

"I don't know dear. Every year brings us more and more children. I have worried for some time that you just can't keep going like this."

Santa worried too. Year after year, he flew faster and faster to make his rounds. To get to every boy and girl on Christmas Eve. How long could it last?

About then, Elf Earl ran into the room. Elf Earl was Santa's special helper.

"Santa, come quick!" Elf Earl was out of breath. He had run all the way from the workshop. "We are all out of paint and there are more toys to finish!" he exclaimed.

Santa quickly put on his heavy coat. Out into the cold and windy night they went. They leaned against the gusting wind. Brrrr! It was a bitter night. Almost 90 degrees below zero!

As they walked toward the workshop, Santa told Earl about his fears. "Earl" Santa said, "They keep bringing us more and more children. Each year my list keeps growing longer and longer."

"Santa, what if the elves helped you?" Santa smiled and patted Earl on the shoulder. He was so very fond of Earl. "You already help Earl. I couldn't do any of this without you."

About then they reached the workshop door. The door almost blew off its hinges as the wind pushed it ahead of Santa and Earl. Whoosh and bang! The heavy door slammed closed behind them.

All the workshop elves crowded around Santa and Earl. "Santa we are out of paint!" cried the Chief Elf. "It is only a week to Christmas and we have all these toys to paint."

"What happened to our paint?" Santa asked patiently. "We thought we had plenty" said the Chief Elf. "Then they brought us these new orders." He held out a large stack of toy orders. "There are just so many more children!"

Santa scratched his head, and then he sighed. "Well, we will have to use part of next year's supply." With that he reached in his pocket and pulled out the big gold key to the storeroom. He gave it to the Chief Elf and then Santa and Elf Earl started back to Santa's house.

Chapter Three—Elf Earl Has A Plan

No sooner were they in the door than Elf Earl excitedly turned to Santa. "I have it!" he exclaimed.

"You have what?" Santa asked.

"I know how we can take care of all the new children." said Elf Earl.

"And just how is that?" asked Santa.

"We will appoint special elf helpers that will go ahead of you. They will do all the work you do now before Christmas Eve. Then on Christmas Eve we will all help you give out the presents." Elf Earl looked very pleased with himself.

"Earl, I don't know" said Santa shaking his head. "The children expect me to be helping them. Will they be happy with my elf helpers?"

"I know they will Santa. They will understand. You will be there on Christmas Eve. Just let me try!" Elf Earl pleaded. Santa looked so tired and worried. Elf Earl had to do something to perk him up. After all, Christmas Eve was only a week away.

"Oh, Santa, let him try." Mrs. Claus had been listening as she finished knitting a pair of woolen mittens. "It might work, and you do need the help."

"All right, all right! I can't hold out against both of you." laughed Santa. It was the first time in days they had heard his special laughter. Mrs. Claus smiled happily and Elf Earl was puffed up with pride. Santa would try his idea.

"Now before you get carried away" Santa said sternly. "I only agree to a test run. Earl you will pick one family and try your idea this week. If it works…"

"Oh, it will, it will!" said the excited Elf.

Santa picked up his list. With his eyes closed, Earl pointed to one name on the list. Mrs. Claus quickly wrote down the name and gave it to Elf Earl.

"Here is your family Earl, Good Luck." said Mrs. Claus. She and Santa started packing for Elf Earl's trip south.

Chapter Four—A Home Far To The South

It was the middle of the night. Exactly one week before Christmas. As Elf Earl peered in the window of the house he saw the two children asleep.

Earl looked at his list. First there was Paige. She was eight years old. This year she wanted…a dollhouse and a bear. Earl looked at her as she snuggled with Tiger, her stuffed animal.

Earl looked again, the next name was Bobby. He was four. He hadn't asked for anything for Christmas yet. Santa had a shiny new train set marked down for him.

As the Elf peered through the frosty window the wind blew and the window rattled. Paige and Bobby both sat up and looked out the window. Before he could move, they spotted him!

"Look" said Paige to her brother. "I told you there were Elves!" She looked very smug. And there wasn't any question. It was an elf. His sharp pointed nose and chin. His fuzzy eyebrows and the biggest ears they had ever seen. They came to a point just under the crown of his cap. Around his neck was a furry jacket collar. His cheeks were red as cherries in spring. His eyes…well, they were black as two lumps of coal.

They ran to the window and opened it quickly. Earl knew he couldn't run away. So he hopped through the window and stood there grinning at them.

"Caught me, yes you did!" he said. Neither one could say a word. Bobby pinched his sister and when she screamed, he knew they were awake.

Elf Earl perched one child on each knee. Then he started to tell them why he was here.

"You see, Santa needs help" he started. "Each year children are added to his list and he just can't be sure of taking care of each one."

Then he told them how the elves planned to help. Earl had been assigned to Paige and Bobby as their special elf. For the next week he would be checking them, listening to their list of toys. He would be doing all the work Santa usually did the week before Christmas.

They wouldn't know he was there…but he would be. And on Christmas Eve he would let them know when Santa was coming so they could be safely in bed.

"How will you tell us Santa is coming Christmas Eve?" Paige asked excitedly. Elf Earl winked and said "that is a secret until Christmas Eve. You will know!"

With that he jumped out of the window into the night. He was gone!

Chapter Five—The Week Of Christmas

All the next week Paige and Bobby were especially good. After all they had really seen an elf and they knew he was watching them. He was their own special elf too!

Once sitting in school, Paige thought she saw him again. Looking through the window. But Earl was too quick for her to get anything but a sneak peek. He was making notes all the time.

Collecting the lists of toys, checking on how good or bad they had been. It was a lot of work. Elf Earl never knew how much Santa went through.

On Saturday, Elf Earl filled in as Santa in the local shopping mall. How he loved picking up the children and listening to them. It didn't matter to him what they wanted. He just liked being with them. He made lots and lots of notes.

Chapter Six—Christmas Eve

Before Elf Earl knew it, the week was up and it was Christmas Eve.

As he helped load Santa's sleigh, Elf Earl told Santa about his week with Paige and Bobby. All Santa did was nod. Earl couldn't tell if he had done well or not.

Lifting off in his sleigh, Santa called back to Elf Earl, "Good luck tonight Earl with Paige and Bobby. We will talk tomorrow. " Then he turned and shouted to the reindeer. They were off!

So was Elf Earl. In his sleigh, he headed straight for Paige and Bobby's house.

He had already violated a chief rule of the elves. No elf was ever to be seen by a child. He knew if he was seen again then Santa would never let him be a Special Elf. And he loved the children and liked helping Santa. It just had to work and he had to be the first of Santa's Special Elves.

Inside the house, Paige and Bobby fretted. They had not had a single sign from Elf Earl since that night. They even began to think it was just a dream.

About then the phone rang. Paige ran to the phone. On the other end was…yes it was…Elf Earl himself.

"I told you I would let you know when Santa was coming. I can never let you see me again but I can, just this once, talk to you. Now listen carefully," Elf Earl said softly, " Sit by the fire after dinner. When you see the fire change colors you will know that Santa is near. Also, there is a special "Santa Alarm" ornament on your tree, and this will start to flash at the same time. Then you must be off to bed, quickly. I will give another signal later for your parents so they too can be in bed before Santa arrives."

Paige and Bobby said not a word. Their eyes were wide and both stared at the fireplace. The fire burned as it usually did. Then they went to the tree and found the special ornament, one they had not seen before. When they went back to the phone, the line was dead. Earl had gone!

Dinner seemed to last forever. At least that night it did. Mother and father kept wondering why the children were looking at the fireplace and then at the Christmas tree. Neither one said a word. After dinner Paige and Bobby ran to the fireplace and sat watching the fire.

The tree was decorated and the family presents were crowded beneath. The stockings were hung from the mantle. Buffy, their dog, lay quietly on the rug by the sofa. Christmas music played. The smell of turkey and dressing filled the house. Father was busy changing lights on the tree and adding wood to the fire.

It was about nine. Paige and Bobby thought nothing was going to happen. But it did! One minute the fire was red and yellow and the next it was bright blue! Then bright green! And on the tree the ornament was flashing!

Paige and Bobby quickly gave Mother and Father big hugs and ran to their room. Mother looked at Father and he just shrugged. They could never get the kids to bed on Christmas Eve. Now they actually ran to bed!

Later, after Mother and Father had checked in on them, Paige and Bobby listened for Santa to come. Once or twice they thought they heard something on the roof. Hooves? Or just tree branches? It was hard to sleep.

Below, Santa and Elf Earl were working quietly around the tree. With Earl's help, Santa quickly put out all the presents. A train for Bobby., A bear and doll-house for Paige. The new dress that Mother had wanted. The tie rack Father had been looking at when Earl spotted him at the mall.

Then, as quickly as he had come, Santa was gone. His sleigh almost empty, heading north again. Behind him was Elf Earl in his sleigh. Across the moon both flew as they headed home for their Christmas.

As they pulled into the sleigh barn at the North Pole, Earl knew that Santa was pleased. Santa jumped down and gave Earl a big Christmas hug.

"Earl, you were right" Santa smiled his broadest and happiest smile. " We can use special elves with the children. Of course I will always be there on Christmas Eve but with your help we can be sure we will reach all the children."

Earl blushed. He was happy and proud.

"Earl, you must start right now for next year. Train our best elves to be my special helpers with the children. Paige and Bobby loved having you as their special elf. The other children will love you too."

So Earl trained his special elves. The next Christmas and every Christmas thereafter the special elves looked after their groups of children. Each had his or her own Special Elf to look after them.

Of course none of the elves ever let the children see them as Elf Earl had done.

As Christmas approaches again this year, Santa and his Special Elves are already hard at work. This year and every year there will be someone special looking out for all the children of the world. No matter how many there are. That makes Elf Earl and Santa very happy indeed.

The End

978-0-595-39747-1
0-595-39747-6